THE WORLD OF DINOSAURS

DIPLODOCUS

BY REBECCA SABELKO

EPIC

BELLWETHER MEDIA · MINNEAPOLIS, MN

D1223007

EPIC BOOKS are no ordinary books. They burst with intense action, high-speed heroics, and shadows of the unknown. Are you ready for an Epic adventure?

This edition first published in 2020 by Bellwether Media, Inc.

No part of this publication may be reproduced in whole or in part without written permission of the publisher. For information regarding permission, write to Bellwether Media, Inc., Attention: Permissions Department, 6012 Blue Circle Drive, Minnetonka, MN 55343.

Library of Congress Cataloging-in-Publication Data

Names: Sabelko, Rebecca, author.
Title: Diplodocus / by Rebecca Sabelko.
Description: Minneapolis, MN : Bellwether Media, Inc., [2020] | Series: Epic: The World of Dinosaurs |
Includes bibliographical references and index. | Audience: Ages 7-12. | Audience: Grades 2 to 7. |
Identifiers: LCCN 2019003727 (print) | LCCN 2019010542 (ebook) |
   ISBN 9781618916594 (ebook) | ISBN 9781644870877 (hardcover : alk. paper) |
   ISBN 9781618917287 (paperback : alk. paper)
Subjects: LCSH: Diplodocus--Juvenile literature.
Classification: LCC QE862.S3 (ebook) | LCC QE862.S3 S2324 2020 (print) | DDC 567.913--dc23
LC record available at https://lccn.loc.gov/2019003727

Editor: Betsy Rathburn   Designer: Jeffrey Kollock

Printed in the United States of America, North Mankato, MN

TABLE OF CONTENTS

THE WORLD OF THE DIPLODOCUS

The diplodocus was a huge dinosaur! It stretched up to 100 feet (30 meters) long. It mostly lived during the Late **Jurassic period**. This was around 160 million years ago!

MAP OF THE WORLD

Late Jurassic period

PRONUNCIATION

dih-PLOD-uh-kus

WHAT WAS THE DIPLODOCUS?

The diplodocus was a **sauropod**. It had a small head and a long neck. The diplodocus had **nostrils** between its eyes. Its teeth were like long pencils!

⚠ ONE LONG DINO!

The diplodocus's neck was around 20 feet (6 meters) long. Its tail was 45 feet (14 meters) long!

⚠ SIZE CHART

25 feet (8 meters)

15 feet (5 meters)

5 feet (2 meters)

The diplodocus was very heavy. Some weighed up to 60,000 pounds (27,216 kilograms).

Four thick legs kept its body steady. Each foot had five toes. One toe on each foot had a sharp claw!

⚠ A HEAVY HEART

The diplodocus heart weighed up to 2,000 pounds (907 kilograms)!

DIET AND DEFENSES

⚠ DIPLODOCUS DIET

leafy
plants

ferns

tree leaves

REACHING GREAT HEIGHTS

The diplodocus often stood on its hind legs to reach leaves on high branches!

The diplodocus could not raise its neck very high. It ate a lot of ground plants. This dinosaur only had front teeth. These teeth **scraped** the leaves from plants.

The diplodocus could only walk around 4 miles (6 kilometers) per hour. But this huge dinosaur did not need to outrun enemies. Only a few **predators** could take the diplodocus down!

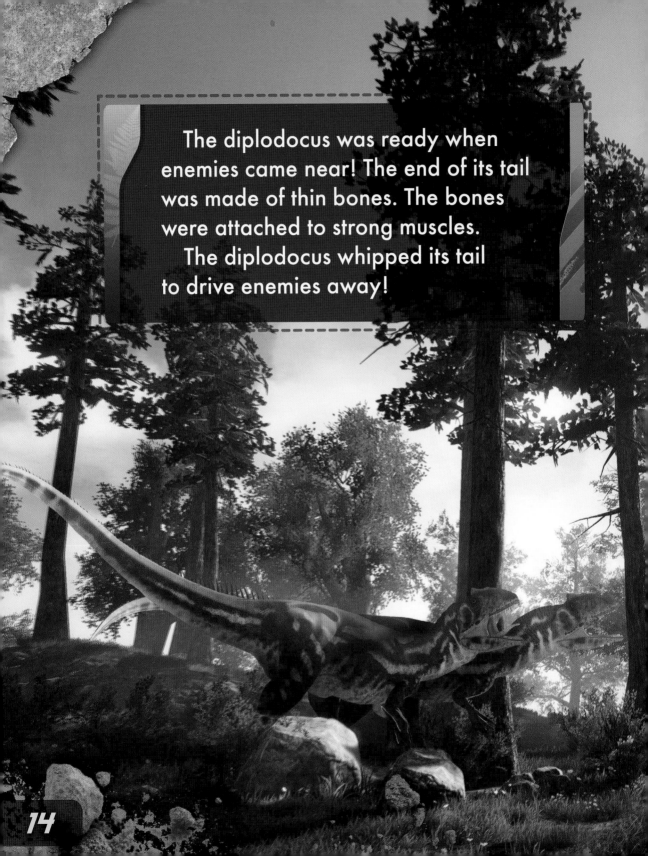

The diplodocus was ready when enemies came near! The end of its tail was made of thin bones. The bones were attached to strong muscles. The diplodocus whipped its tail to drive enemies away!

⚠ THE BARE BONES

The diplodocus had hollow neck, back, and tail bones. This made it much lighter than other dinosaurs its size.

FOSSILS AND EXTINCTION

The diplodocus went **extinct** about 154 million years ago.

Some scientists think new animals **evolved** from the diplodocus. Others believe **climate** changes made it hard for the dinosaur's food to grow.

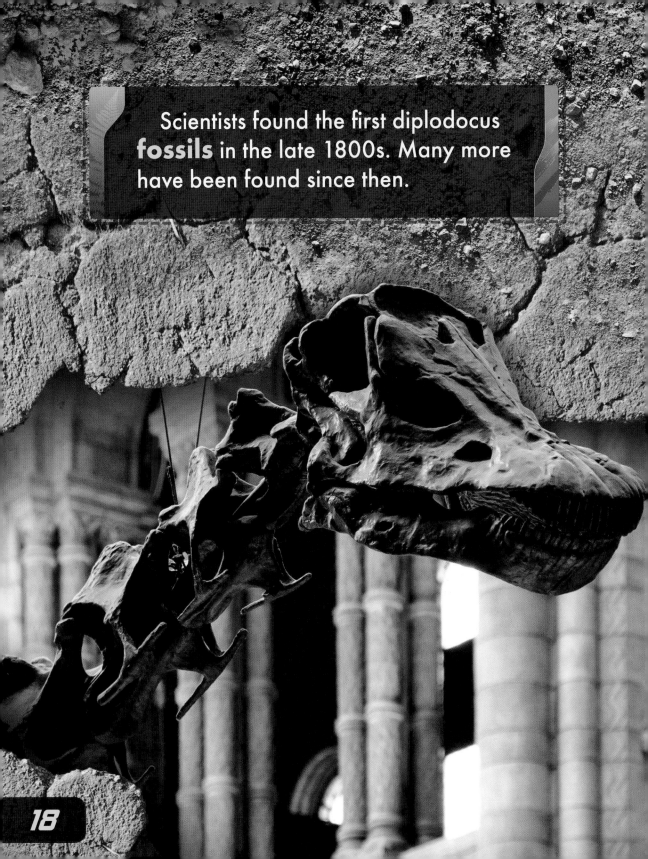

Scientists found the first diplodocus **fossils** in the late 1800s. Many more have been found since then.

DIPLODOCUS FOSSIL MAP

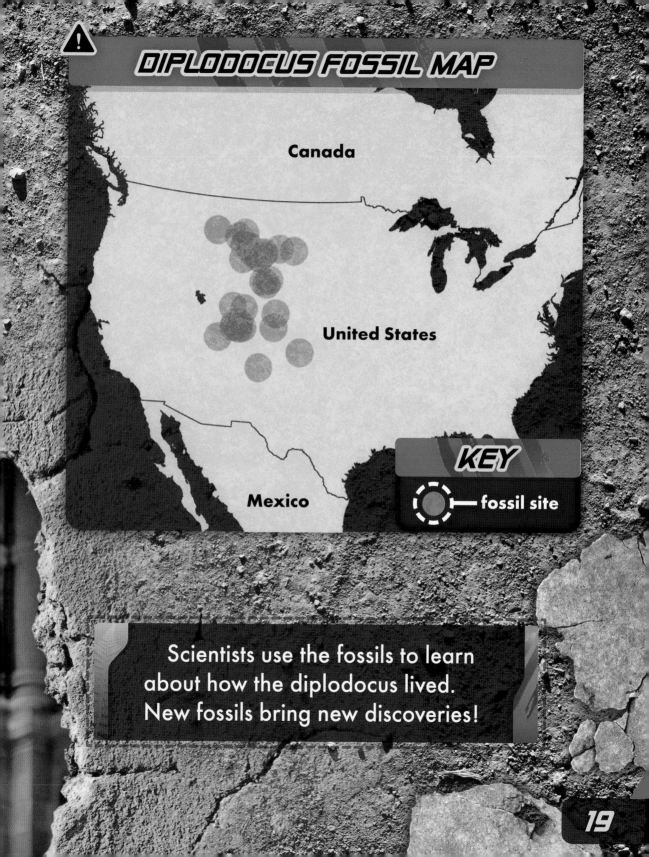

Canada

United States

Mexico

KEY

O----fossil site

Scientists use the fossils to learn about how the diplodocus lived. New fossils bring new discoveries!

GET TO KNOW THE DIPLODOCUS

⚠️ **FIRST FOSSILS FOUND**

1877 in Morrison Formation
near Cañon City, Colorado

HEIGHT up to 15 feet (5 meters) tall at the shoulder

long tail

⚠️ **LOCATION**

North America

thick leg

LENGTH up to 100 feet (30 meters) long

ERA 163 million to 145 million years ago during the Late Jurassic period

Triassic   Jurassic   Cretaceous

long neck

FOUND BY

Benjamin Mudge and Samuel Williston

small head

FOOD

leafy plants   tree leaves

WEIGHT   up to 60,000 pounds (27,216 kilograms)

=

GLOSSARY

climate—the usual weather conditions in a certain place

evolved—changed slowly, often into a better, more complex state

extinct—no longer living

fossils—the remains of living things that lived long ago

Jurassic period—the second period of the Mesozoic era that occurred between 200 million and 145 million years ago; the Late Jurassic period began around 163 million years ago.

nostrils—the openings of the nose

predators—animals that hunt other animals for food

sauropod—a four-legged dinosaur that ate plants and lived during the Jurassic and Cretacous periods; sauropods had small heads and long necks and tails.

scraped—removed from a plant by rubbing teeth against it

TO LEARN MORE

AT THE LIBRARY

Hansen, Grace. *Diplodocus*. Minneapolis, Minn.: Abdo Kids, 2018.

Hibbert, Clare. *Giant Dinosaurs: Sauropods*. New York, N.Y.: Enslow Publishing, 2018.

Hirsch, Rebecca E. *Diplodocus*. Lake Elmo, Minn.: Focus Readers, 2018.

ON THE WEB

FACTSURFER

Factsurfer.com gives you a safe, fun way to find more information.

1. Go to www.factsurfer.com.

2. Enter "diplodocus" into the search box and click 🔍.

3. Select your book cover to see a list of related web sites.

INDEX